Printed in China by WKT Co. Ltd. on FSC-certified paper.

Manufactured in China, May 2025
This product conforms to CPSIA 2008

ISBN 978-1-63158-732-0

Text and illustrations copyright © b small publishing 2025

First Racehorse for Young Readers Edition 2025

All rights reserved. No part of this book may be reproduced in any manner without the express written consent of the publisher, except in the case of brief excepts in critical reviews or articles. All inquiries should be addressed to Racehorse for Young Readers, 307 West 36th Street, 11th Floor, New York, NY 10018.

Racehorse for Young Readers books may be purchased in bulk at special discounts for sales promotions, corporate gifts, fund-raising or education purposes. Special editions can also be created to specifications. For details, contact the Special Sales Department at Skyhorse Publishing, 307 West 36th Street, 11th Floor, New York, NY 10018 or info@skyhorsepublishing.com.

Racehorse for Young Readers® is a registered trademark of Skyhorse Publishing, Inc.®, a Delaware corporation.

Visit our website at www.skyhorsepublishing.com.

Creative Director: Vicky Barker
Editorial: Alice Harman

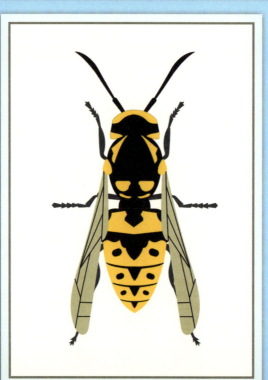

WHAT IS ENTOMOLOGY?

Entomology is the area of science that studies insects. It is a branch of biology. Scientists who specialize in entomology are called entomologists. They investigate what insects look like, how they behave, and where they live.

WHAT IS STEM?

STEM stands for "science, technology, engineering, and mathematics." These four areas are closely linked, and entomology uses skills from all four of them. If we understand how insects live, we can help protect them and maybe even learn from them.

Science   Technology   Engineering   Math

FIRST THINGS FIRST!

People often use the word **bug** when talking about an insect. They're not always wrong! But they're not always right either...

Bugs belong to a group of insects called **Hemiptera.** Entomologists call them **true bugs,** and they include bedbugs, cicadas, and aphids.

All insects in this group have a long snout for piercing animal skin or leaves. Then they suck up or taste the juices! If an insect is not in this group, it is not technically a '"bug."

IDENTIFYING INSECTS

Hemiptera is only one of many groups of insects. These groups are known as **orders**. Entomologists are always discovering new things so it's hard to say exactly how many orders there are.

Many of the orders get their names from Greek words. Hemiptera means "half wing." This name comes from these insects' first pair of wings, which are usually half hard and half soft.

Can you match these insects with their order, based on the Greek definition? Answers on page 30.

Lepidoptera (scale-winged)

Coleoptera (sheath-winged)*

Hymenoptera (membrane-winged)**

Orthoptera (straight-winged)

* A sheath is like a case or a cover.

** A membrane is a thin barrier.

WINGS!

Many insects are able to fly, and they often have two pairs of wings. But not all insects follow this rule. The most famous flying insect—the fly!—has only one pair of wings. A beetle's outer pair of wings are hard and don't help them to fly. Instead, they protect the softer wings underneath.

Being able to fly is one of the reasons that insects survive so well in nature. They can escape danger, find food, meet other insects, and look for the perfect home.

SIX OR EIGHT

Insects usually have six legs, all on their **thorax.** This is also where insects' wings are, if they have them. Many people think that spiders are insects but we know that spiders famously have eight legs. They are not insects! They are **arachnids.**

An insect's head comes before its thorax, and its **abdomen** is at the back.

Can you match these functions to the part of the insect where they happen? Answers on page 31.

Functions: ▸ Eating ▸ Going to the bathroom ▸ Digesting food ▸ Seeing ▸ Smelling ▸ Moving ▸ Flying ▸ Biting ▸ Stinging

Head	Thorax	Abdomen
_____	_____	_____
_____	_____	_____
_____	_____	_____
_____	_____	_____
_____	_____	_____
_____	_____	_____

YOU'VE CHANGED!

An insect begins its life as an egg. Most insect eggs hatch into **larvae** that look nothing like the grown-up version of that insect. For example, a butterfly egg hatches into a caterpillar! That caterpillar is called a **larva** ("larvae" is the plural word). Before it becomes a butterfly, it has to eat lots of food and then turn into a **pupa**.

Not all insects go through this **larval** stage, but most of them do. Some insects, such as grasshoppers, go from egg to **nymph** to adult. The nymph looks like a smaller version of the adult.

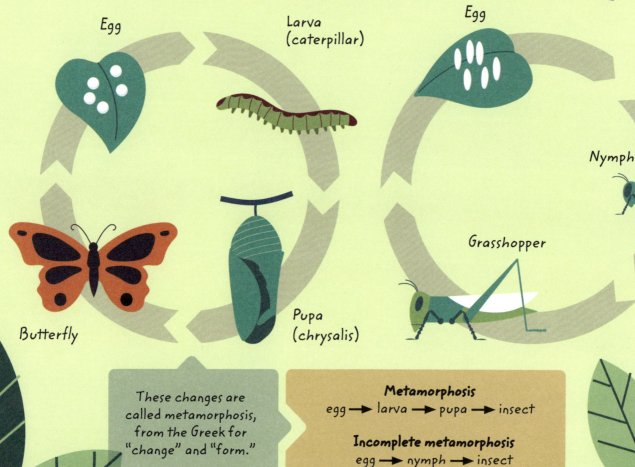

Egg

Larva (caterpillar)

Egg

Nymph

Grasshopper

Butterfly

Pupa (chrysalis)

These changes are called metamorphosis, from the Greek for "change" and "form."

Metamorphosis
egg ➔ larva ➔ pupa ➔ insect

Incomplete metamorphosis
egg ➔ nymph ➔ insect

Can you find all the words from the orange box in this word search? Words can read backwards, forwards, up, down, and diagonally. Answers on page 31.

> Each group of insects has a specific type of pupa. A butterfly's pupa is called a chrysalis, and for a mosquito it's called a tumbler.

```
g t h f d e r p i a t s u b
y o n u p n t c r t l q j r
k f y l f r e t t u b e c f
r n o i a r u b l m o h g u
e v m r c r i t r b r a e a
p s a e e x v o u l e d s i d l g
p k s t t s q a e e n g h l r e b
o i w g b a t n e r d e l m a u a
h e p x y g m e l h p m y n i h h
s q o r i o p o s i o v u c n n s
s v t o l c s i r g g r u b f e y
a s p a c a t e r p i l l a r t k
r t j u g b r k o t h w t n r t s
g p l g s a f r s z h o a i e u t
w y e e o l w u s i l a s y r h c
s h i m f l a m y r p h w i g e a
f e t p u p a s e o g m e l s e b
```

| metamorphosis | pupa | chrysalis | egg | butterfly |
| larvae | nymph | tumbler | caterpillar | grasshopper |

LIGHT IT UP

While an insect's small size helps it survive in nature, it can make it hard to find other insects of the same kind. The firefly has found a clever solution! It can make its abdomen glow with a cold light that it can flash on and off. Fireflies use these flashes to communicate, helping them find others of the same **species** (or type).

Fireflies do this by controlling a clever chemical reaction in their bodies. The main reason for finding each other is to reproduce and make more fireflies!

Can you spot the odd one out in each row?
Answers on page 31.

WATCH OUT!

Insects are a good source of protein in the natural world. To avoid being eaten, some insects have evolved to be very brightly colored. Red, orange, black, or yellow often mean "Danger!" in the human world. It's the same for insects.

The Hibiscus harlequin bug is bright orange and shiny. Its natural predators, birds, see those colors and think that it is probably poisonous so they leave it alone. This bug isn't actually poisonous but the warning colors have tricked the birds!

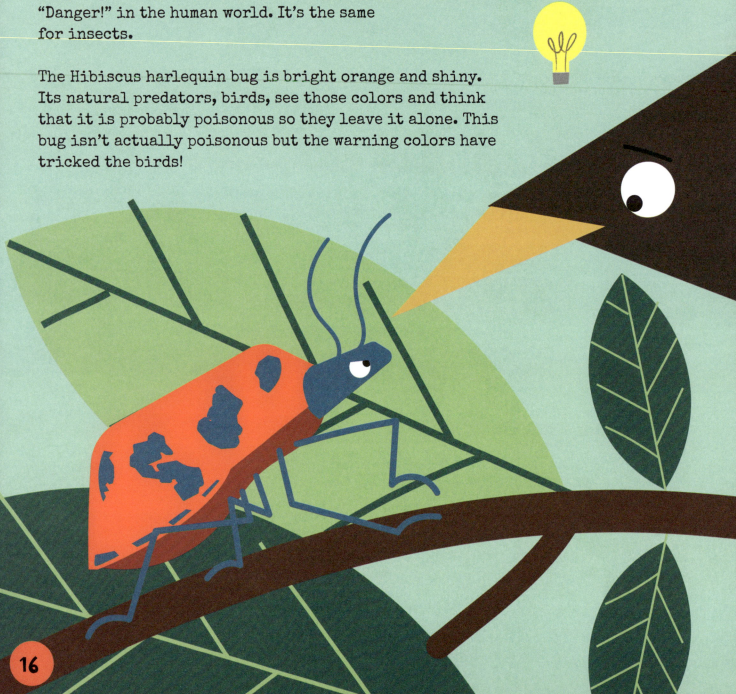

Complete the drawing and then color in this insect with big, bright, bold warning colors.

MORE THAN CAMOUFLAGE

You've probably heard of camouflage, where an animal blends into its surroundings. Well, insects have taken this a step further! Some insects blend in so convincingly that it's almost impossible to see them. This is called **mimicry**.

Leaf insects and stick insects do this very well. Can you guess what they hide as?

How many leaf insects and stick insects can you count hiding in this scene?
Answers on page 31.

LOOK WHO'S TALKING

Male cicadas try to attract female cicadas with loud noises. An African species of cicada known as *Brevisana brevis* is on record as the loudest insect ever! It can make a sound that is over 100 **decibels,** which is about as loud as a hairdryer.

Bees are also famous for making noise - they buzz! This buzzing comes from their wings, which can beat over **230 times** per second.

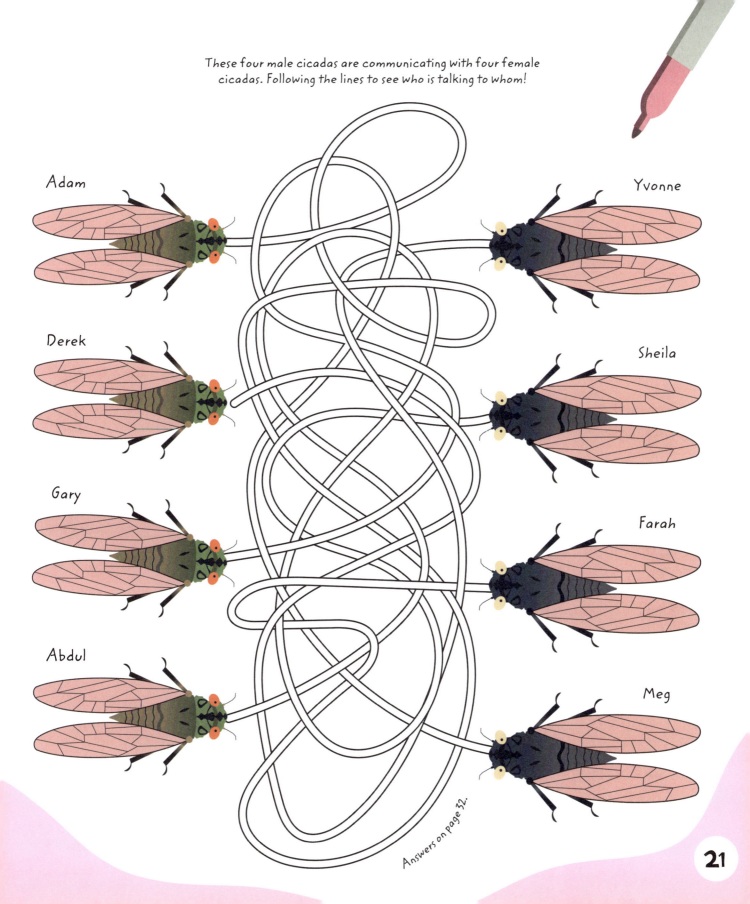

AMAZING HOMES

Ants live in complex nests known as **colonies**. Each colony has at least one queen, who lays all the eggs. Most of the other ants are workers. Like humans, ants are very social, and they thrive living together.

Unlike humans, ants can't talk. So how do they get along? They release chemicals that other ants detect with their **antennae**. Ants can work together in a team to fight off big predators or make decisions about how to build their colony. Ant-mazing!

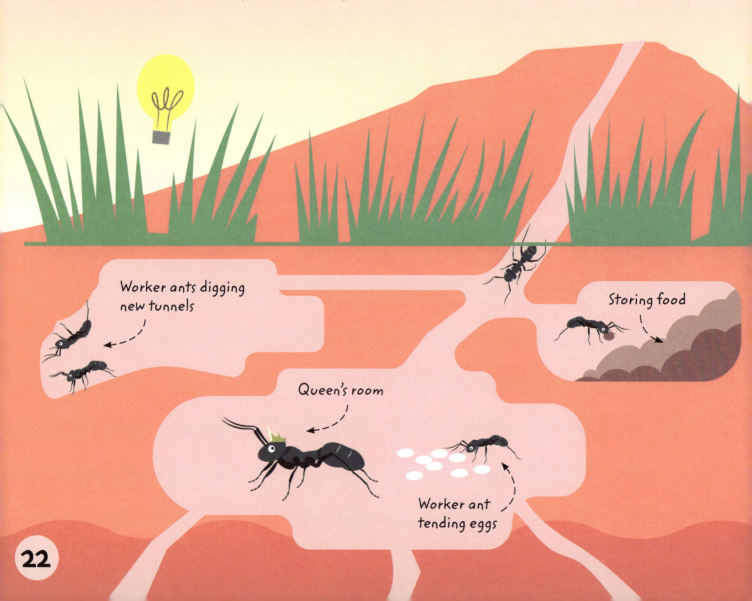

Worker ants digging new tunnels

Storing food

Queen's room

Worker ant tending eggs

Design your own ant colony! It might include a room for the queen, another room for future queens, somewhere to store food and a place to raise the babies. Maybe even a room to rest in! What else would you want to add?

HELPING US OUT

They may not be doing it on purpose but insects are helpful to humans. In fact, they are essential to life on Earth! Bees fly around looking for **pollen** to feed to their larvae. They also collect **nectar** to feed to other bees. Bees store carry the pollen in little pockets on their back legs, called **corbiculae**.

When bees buzz from flower to flower, pollen catches on their bodies and then rubs off on other plants. This pollen transfer is how plants reproduce, giving us fruit, vegetables, and animal feed. Without bees, we'd have no food to eat!

Find the group of bees and flowers that matches the one on the right.
Answers on page 32.

UNEXPECTED FRIENDS

We know that bees are important to our food system but what about their less popular cousins, wasps? While bees are busy pollinating flowers, wasps are busy eating the caterpillars and greenfly that like to eat plants. This keeps their numbers down and lets the plants grow!

Wasps drink nectar from flowers so they can also be accidental pollinators, carrying the pollen from flower to flower.

Can you spot the ten differences between these garden scenes?
Answers on page 32.

LOOK AROUND YOU

There are around 1 million different types of insects that we know about, but entomologists believe there are many millions more not yet discovered. If it's safe to do so where you live, you can place a square on the ground and study which insects and other minibeasts move in and out of it.

Follow the instructions to make your own frame
to study the insects where you live.

What you will need! → A piece of paper → A pair of scissors

1. Fold a piece of paper in half.

2. Cut out a square from the folded side to make a frame.

3. Place the frame on the ground in a safe place (ask an adult to help you choose) and watch it for 15 minutes. How many insects can you identify?

Draw or write your discoveries here!
Try to identify the creatures using a book,
or a website or app that you know is safe to use.

ANSWERS

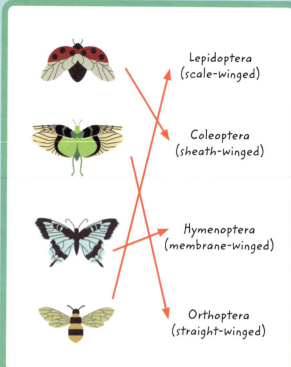

page 7

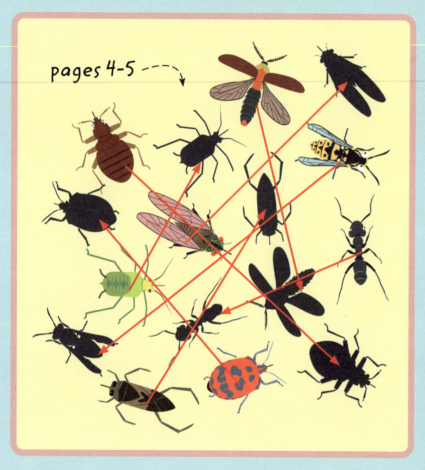

pages 4-5

Bugs
1. Bedbug
2. Aphid
4. Cicada
5. Hibiscus Harlequin Bug
6. Water boatman

Non-bugs
3. Firefly
7. Wasp
8. Ant

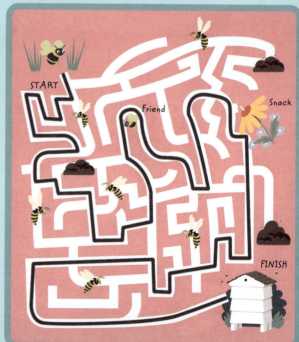

page 9

page 11

Head
Eating
Seeing
Smelling
Biting

Thorax
Digesting food
Moving
Flying

Abdomen
Going to the bathroom
Stinging

page 13

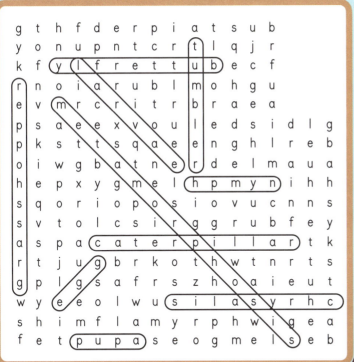

page 15

page 19

8 leaf insects
8 stick insects

page 21

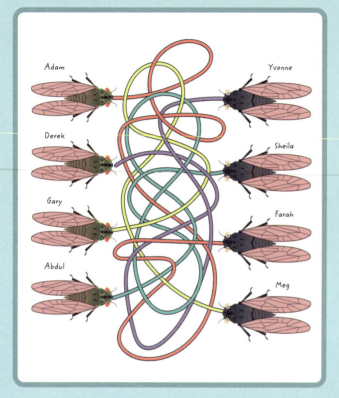

page 25

page 27